We Exalt Thee

PRAISE AND WORSHIP FAVORITES IN TWO PARTS

Arranged by

MARTY PARKS

Lillenas PUBLISHING COMPANY
KANSAS CITY, MO 64141

CONTENTS

All Hail King Jesus

with
Crown Him King of Kings

Words and Music by
DAVE MOODY
Arranged by Marty Parks

All hail King Je - sus. All hail Em -

8

CD: 3

*"Crown Him King of Kings"

I will reign with Him.

Crown Him King of Kings, crown Him Lord of Lords,

Won-der-ful, Coun-sel-or, the Might-y God;

Em - man - u - el, God is

with us, and He shall reign,

CD: 4

None like You

We Will Honor Your Name with Praise
I Worship You, Almighty God

Arranged by Marty Parks

*"We Will Honor Your Name with Praise"

"I Worship You, Almighty God"

I wor-ship You, Al-mighty God; there is none like You. I wor-ship You, O Prince of Peace; that is what I

praise.

Because We Believe

Words and Music by
JAMIE HARVILL
and NANCY GORDON
Arranged by Marty Parks

We be-lieve____ in____

21

wor - thy is our King!

All glo - ry___ and hon - or___ are

His to___ re - ceive;_____ To Je - sus___ we

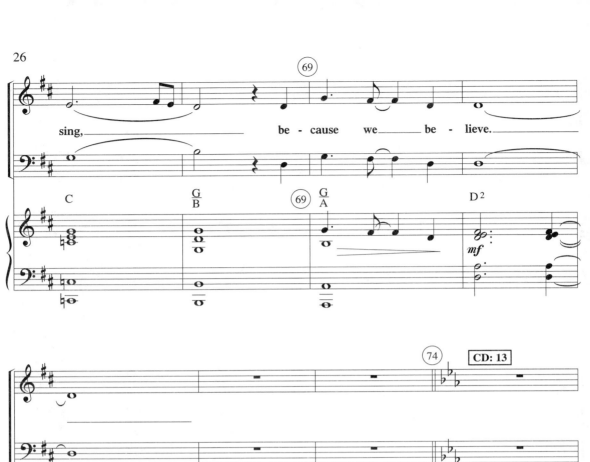

sing,_____ be - cause we___ be - lieve.___

We be - lieve___ in the

CD: 14

To be-come the Bride of Christ.

Ho - ly, ho - ly, ho - ly

is our God!

His to re - ceive; To

Je - sus we sing, Be -

cause we be - lieve. Because we be -

The Love of Christ

Words and Music by
MARTY PARKS
Arranged by Marty Parks

How— long,————— how— wide,————— how— deep,—

————— how— high————— Is the love of Christ,—————

the love of Christ. How long,

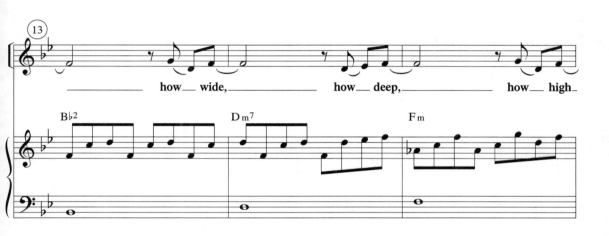

how wide, how deep, how high

Is the love of Christ, the love of

The Greatest Thing

with
I Exalt Thee

Words and Music by
MARK PENDERGRASS
Arranged by Marty Parks

44

gods.

For Thou, O Lord, art high a-bove all the earth; Thou art ex-

alt - ed far a-bove all gods.

CD: 26

Shout to the Lord

Words and Music by
DARLENE ZSCHECH
Arranged by Marty Parks

56

CD: 32 2nd time

2nd time to Coda ⊕
(to pg. 60, meas. 59)

2nd time to Coda ⊕
(to pg. 60, meas. 59)

will roar _____ at the sound _____ of Your

name._____ I sing for joy____ at the work ____

___ of Your hands,_____ For- ev- er I'll love____ You, for- ev-

God Is the Strength of My Heart

Words and Music by
EUGENE GRECO
Arranged by Marty Parks

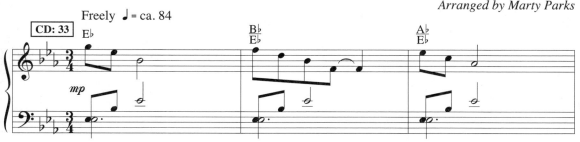

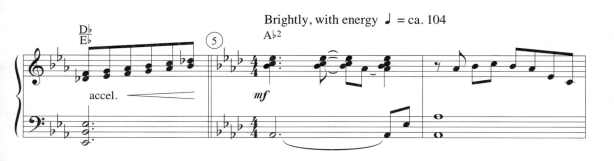

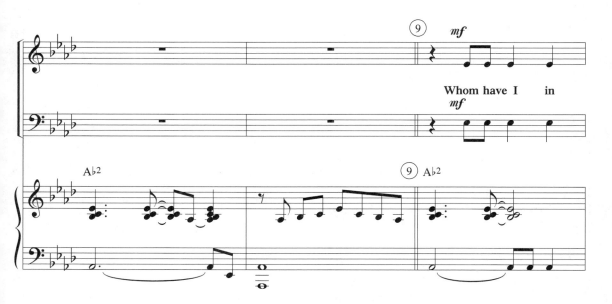

PLEASE NOTE: Copying of this product is not covered by CCLI licenses. For CCLI information call 1-800-234-2446.

My heart and my strength, man - y times___ they fail,

But there is one Truth that

al - ways will___ pre - vail: God is the strength___

D.S. al Coda
(to pg. 66, meas. 26)

CD: 36

72

The Reason I Live

In Moments like These
When I Look into Your Holiness

Arranged by Marty Parks

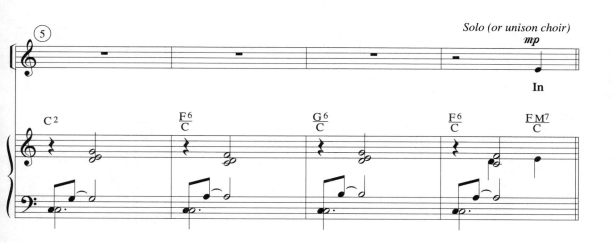

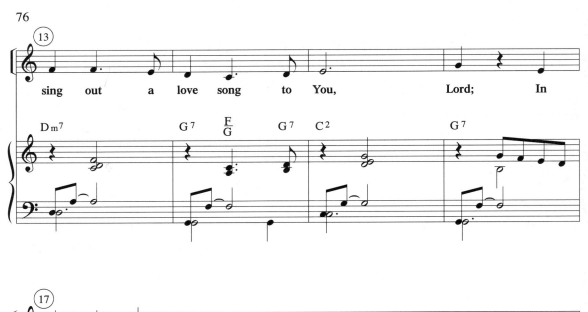

sing out a love song to You, Lord; In

mo - ments like these, I lift up my hands, I

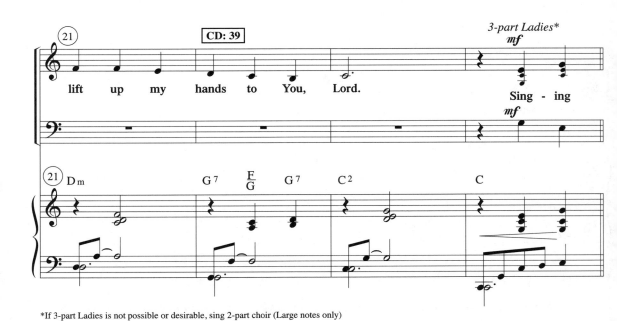

lift up my hands to You, Lord. Sing - ing

*If 3-part Ladies is not possible or desirable, sing 2-part choir (Large notes only)

Our Great and Mighty God

What a Mighty God We Serve
Great and Mighty Is He
Mighty Is Our God

Arranged by Marty Parks

-er name; His pow'r is great - er,_____ for

He has cre - at - ed ev - ery-thing.

Might-y is_____ our God,_____ might-y is_____ our King;_____

CD: 49

Sovereign Lord

with

How Great Is He

Words and Music by
TOM FETTKE
Arranged by Marty Parks

*"How Great Is He"

1st time: Solo (opt. unison choir)
2nd time: Choir

How great is He, How strong and might - y! King of Kings, Lord of Lords, E - ter - nal God.

Come into the Holy of Holies

with
Holy Is the Lord

Words and Music by
JOHN SELLERS
Arranged by Marty Parks

Come in - to His pres - ence with sing - - ing,_____

CD: 56

Wor - ship at the throne_____ of God._____

Ladies unison

Come in - to the Ho - ly of Ho - lies,_____

Men unison

Come in - to the Ho - ly of Ho - ly -

*"Holy Is the Lord"

You Will Always Be (Ancient of Days)

Words and Music by
MARTY PARKS
Arranged by Marty Parks

CD: 60   Mysteriously ♩ = ca. 72

*WORSHIP LEADER: Sovereign Lord, You have made the heavens and the earth by Your

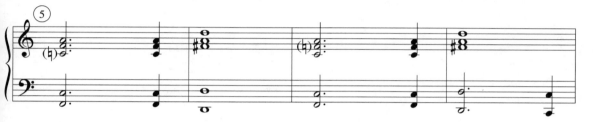

outstretched arm. Nothing is too difficult for You! You are worthy, Lord, to receive glory

and honor and power, for You have created all things. By Your will and for Your pleasure

they were created! *(adapted from Jeremiah 32:17 and Revelation 4:11)*

All be-long___ to You, An - cient of Days! Al - might - y God! Lord___ of All!